Old Time Revivals

Old Time Revivals

INSIGHTS INTO THE GREAT 18TH & 19TH CENTURIES REVIVALS

JOHN SHEARER

We enjoy hearing from our readers. Please contact us at www.anekopress.com/questions-comments with any questions, comments, or suggestions.

Old Time Revivals

© 2024 by Aneko Press

All rights reserved. First edition 1927.

Revisions copyright 2024.

Please do not reproduce, store in a retrieval system, or transmit in any form or by any means – electronic, mechanical, photocopying, recording, or otherwise, without written permission from the publisher. Please contact us via www.AnekoPress.com for reprint and translation permissions.

Scripture quotations from The Authorized (King James) Version. Rights in the Authorized Version in the United Kingdom are vested in the Crown. Reproduced by permission of the Crown's patentee, Cambridge University Press.

Cover Designer: J. Martin

Cover Background: iStock/Apostrophes

Editor: Paul Miller

Aneko Press

www.anekopress.com

Aneko Press, Life Sentence Publishing, and our logos are trademarks of

Life Sentence Publishing, Inc.
203 E. Birch Street
P.O. Box 652
Abbotsford, WI 54405

RELIGION / Christian Church / History

Paperback ISBN: 979-8-88936-433-7

eBook ISBN: 979-8-88936-434-4

10   9   8   7   6   5   4   3   2   1

Available where books are sold

Contents

Chapter 1

The Puritan Revival

The story of the Puritan Revival is that of England itself in the most heroic period of her history. It is the story of her great uncrowned king, Oliver Cromwell. It is the story of an earnest and sustained endeavor to found the government of this realm upon the deep, broad base of the Eternal Righteousness. It is the story of a time when, in the glowing language of Richard Baxter, "England was like to become a land of saints, a pattern of holiness to the world, and the unmatchable paradise of the earth."

The story of the Puritan Revival is all this because it is the story of the English Bible. The real beginnings of Puritanism are seen in London when, as the fruit of the sacrificial labors of William Tyndale and his brethren, the Book of God was at last given to the people in their own tongue. The first six Bibles were set up in the church of St. Paul's, and day after day

William Tyndale

crowds flocked to the edifice to drink from the living stream. Good readers were in great request, and one of these men, John Porter, stands out vividly in the page of the historian. Porter was a fresh young man, big of stature, to whom the multitude resorted "because he could read well and had an audible voice." Soon that glad and solemn scene was repeated throughout the whole land, for in every parish church the Bible was displayed, chained in the chapel, and, as in the days of Nehemiah, people listened with streaming eyes to the words of the Book.

But the Book did not remain in the churches. In the form of the small Genevan version, it entered the homes of the people, and there it was deeply and prayerfully pondered. It is good that it was so, for the clergy of that day, before the Puritan Revival reached the pulpit, were faithless shepherds, and in many cases were dreadfully immoral. In Baxter's parish, the vicar, an old blind man, pastoring two churches twenty miles apart, never preached at all, but repeated the prayers by heart (and without heart!), being assisted eventually by his son, the best stage actor and gambler in the area. Sunday was a day of revelry. The Morris dancers, in their wild attire, entered the church, gave careless heed to the mumbled devotions, and then ran out to play. But quietly and surely, the Bible did its divine work in the homes of the people. As they read, men and women everywhere were awakened and converted.

These converts of the pure Word were marked at once as a distinct people. A deep sense of the holy majesty of God possessed them. An inexpressible light seemed to spring from the Book and fill them. The awesome purity of God, contrasting with the corrupt world around them, almost overwhelmed their spirit. It entered into them and filled them with a tremendous earnestness of moral purpose. It is no wonder that they appeared to their neighbors as inhabitants of another realm. People tried to find a name for them, and as often before and since, the nickname they invented stuck fast. They called them Puritans.

In other days Puritanism might have held on in its quiet channels, awakening the nation by a gently pervasive influence, but the course of events brought it into a great and considerable prominence. Because of the decisive part it played in the English Civil War, we are inclined to think of it as essentially stern and warlike; but in truth, Puritanism found its strength in a quiet and peaceable people. They suffered long and patiently under the cruel tyranny of the Stuarts. Rather than lift the sword against their unworthy rulers, a multitude sought refuge in the New World, and battling with nature's grim but honest powers, they built up a free and righteous state. In the course of about ten years, twenty thousand of the best of England's race crossed the Atlantic Ocean, and the great American commonwealth is the direct outcome of the Puritan awakening. From the days of the Pilgrim Fathers, America has been the home of revival, and there the living waters have again and again appeared to diffuse a worldwide blessing.

In England itself, a strange and wonderful time followed the triumph of Oliver Cromwell and the Puritan host. By the Solemn League and Covenant, the nation bound itself to God in holy obedience. The Bible was placed on the table of the House of Commons and recognized as the source of its laws and the inspiration of its life. Active godliness became the indispensable qualification for public office. Swearing, drunkenness, and impurity were criminal offences. Every theater in the land was closed. England became a refuge of the oppressed, the tower and strength of Protestantism in Europe. It never stood higher among the nations than in the days of Cromwell's Protectorate.

These were the days of the great Puritan preachers – of John Owen, John Howe, Richard Baxter, Thomas Goodwin, and John Bunyan, whose works have enriched every generation of preachers since, and whose pastoral devotion has never been surpassed. In a brief account of one of these we may taste the quality of a Puritan minister and feel the power of the Puritan Revival. When Richard Baxter went to Kidderminster, it had a population of about three thousand shrewd, hardheaded weavers who worked diligently and lived in considerable comfort. Their vicar was a weak, incompetent man who preached only once a quarter, and then so foolishly that he stirred up only the laughter of his audience, while his assistant was a common drunkard seldom out of the tavern, and ignorant even of the Children's Catechism. The people, thus neglected, abode in deep spiritual darkness and were ignorant, wild, and ungodly.

When Richard Baxter settled among them, they gave him a rough reception, but the completely selfless spirit of the man soon secured their respect. He possessed one of the finest intellects of the time. He was a master of mathematics, physics, and medicine. But the entire lot of his knowledge, the whole being of the man, was aglow with the love of God and for his fellow men. His whole energy flowed in one channel. He was always and everywhere a soul winner. He preached with passionate earnestness, and always, he tells us, "as a dying man to dying men." Soon the large church was filled to overflowing, and gallery after gallery had to be added, until there were five.

How often is the pastor lost in the preacher! Baxter felt that his work was only half done when he had studiously prepared and forcefully preached his sermon. He must come into vital, personal, individual touch with his people, and so he developed his own method of catechizing. He arranged for every family in his parish to come to his house, one by one, and he spent an hour with each family. Then he took each member individually, and he urgently, tenderly urged each person to make an immediate decision for Christ. Seldom did a family leave Baxter's door without tears. The fruit of this labor was most precious, and it filled the faithful minister's heart with an overflowing joy. Fully a third of the older inhabitants were converted, and the young received a great blessing. Family worship was set up in almost every home, and as one passed through the streets, the songs of Zion might be heard resounding from every quarter. Kidderminster became a "colony of heaven" in the days of the Puritans. The blessing spread to the surrounding areas. The neighboring ministers especially felt the heavenly influence, and Baxter became a shepherd of shepherds to his brethren. *The Reformed Pastor*, that great Puritan writing, contains the essence of his instructions, and it has inspired and directed some of the noblest ministries of modern times. This book and his *Call to the Unconverted*, along with *The Saints' Everlasting Rest*, are his abiding legacy to the church.[1]

---

1   *The Reformed Pastor* and *A Call to the Unconverted* are available from Aneko Press.

Richard Baxter

Chapter 2

A Great Day at Kirk of Shotts

John Livingston was born in the manse of Kilsyth in 1603. He was one of those happy souls who can never date their second birth. Claimed for God in his infancy by the mighty faith of his parents, reared in a home that shone with the beauty of holiness, he could never remember a time when he did not love God and want to please Him. In his school days he was a member of the church at Stirling, and never did a communicant approach the Lord's Table in a more appropriate frame. A holy awe came upon him that made his very body tremble, but soon sweet comfort and assurance came to this lamb of the Good Shepherd. He fervently desired to serve Christ, and at first he thought he could best do so as a physician. But one day as he meditated in a cave by the Mouse Water River, God spoke and called the lad. He left the cave with the conviction that one path alone lay open to him. He must serve in the ministry of the gospel.

He prepared himself at Glasgow College, and in 1625, at Stewarton, he began to preach Christ. The true church was quick to recognize the grace of God in him, and in many places his pastoral services were eagerly sought. But everywhere the bishop forbade his settlement. His warm evangelism was highly offensive to the "moderate" palate, and so young Livingston entered the furnace. For five long years he remained there. It was a heavy trial. With a heart hungering to preach Christ, and with fields of service invitingly opened before him, he was held back by the grim hand of the royal episcopate. But, though he did not know it, God's hand was quietly overruling the enemy's purpose and refining him for a glorious task.

Now we have to note, as so often before in the story of revival, how God made use of a seemingly fortunate circumstance to further His great purpose of grace. It happened that some ladies of high rank, who mourned in secret the decline of the Reformed faith, were traveling in the neighborhood of Shotts when their carriage broke down. The accident took place beside the manse. The minister, Mr. Hance, hurried out and invited them to take shelter under his roof until the repairs were completed. They gladly did so, and seeing that the minister's house was sadly dilapidated, and indeed in a still more unsafe state than their carriage, they returned his kindness soon afterward by building a new manse in a better situation. Kindness begets kindness. When Mr. Hance waited upon the ladies to thank them, he asked if there was anything he could do to express his gratitude. Then they ventured to make a bold request – a request that was the real outcome of their private prayers. Would he open his church at the coming sacrament to some of the persecuted ministers, whom they named? Mr. Hance at once consented, and among those named was the young man, John Livingston.

The communion was set for June 20, 1630. Great interest was awakened, and a vast assembly was gathered together from all parts. Rich blessing followed the Word at the Sunday services – so rich indeed that it was felt they could not part without an added day of thanksgiving. It was on this added day that God poured out the superabundant blessing. After much persuasion, Livingston consented to preach the next day. Finding their hearts too full of joy for sleep, many people formed themselves into little groups and spent the whole night in fervent devotion, in praise and supplication. The young preacher was in one of these praying groups, and when the morning came, a serious trial troubled him. As he thought of the great, expectant multitude, he was overwhelmed by a sense of utter unworthiness, incompetence, and insufficiency. All strength seemed to leave him, and he was brought down to the dust of death. So real and painful was the dejection that he gave up all thought of preaching, and he was preparing to sneak away through the fields when his friends gathered around him and convinced him to remain.

And so, on June 21, in the churchyard of Shotts, John Livingston stood up among the people, feeling himself the weakest and least of God's creatures. Then was fulfilled the saying of the prophet Hosea, *When Ephraim spake trembling, he exalted himself in Israel* (Hosea 13:1). God uplifted him and perfected His strength in the young man's weakness. His text was Ezekiel 36:25-26: *Then will I sprinkle clean water upon you and ye shall be clean. . . . A new heart also will I give you, and a new spirit will I put within you.* As he expounded the Bible passage, burning thoughts and burning words filled his heart and lips. For an hour and a half, he preached to a people who seemed rooted to the ground in a great stillness. Then, when he thought he must end, again the Spirit filled him with a fulness that must be outpoured, and for another hour he continued with a melting of heart and liberty of utterance he never experienced before or after. Five hundred men and women, some from the high ranks of society, and some poor vagabonds and beggars, were converted where they stood, and from that day on lived as those who had indeed received a new heart and a new spirit. The memory of that day has never died, and the very telling of its story, as at Kilsyth, has proved to be a fount of revival.

Chapter 3

The Great Awakening

The eighteenth century opened for England in deep spiritual gloom. The Puritan Revival was almost extinct, and a cold deism, that hardly troubled to disguise itself, reigned in the church. A manifest darkness covered the people. The court was corrupt. Sin walked naked and unashamed. In the high circles of government, bribery had become a fine art. It was a day of cynical timeservers. In many parts of the country, the people had relapsed into simple depravity. England, indeed, was not far from the abyss when she was suddenly rescued, uplifted, and launched upon a career of glorious victory and expansion by the great evangelical awakening. In the judgment of even the rationalist historian, England was saved and, as it were, reborn by this great movement of the divine Spirit.

It was at Oxford University that the new life first appeared, but if we search deeply, we will find its hidden spring in the heart of a praying mother. In truth, revival is largely the story of praying mothers. Susannah Wesley, wife of the rector of Epworth, is one of the great women of the church, and her devoted indomitable spirit had a deep and abiding influence upon the founder of Methodism. In 1730 we find John Wesley as the leader of a little band of sincere young men who gave themselves to prayer, the Bible, and works of charity. In derision, people called them the Holy Club and Bible moths; then, observing that they were very exact and methodical in their habits, named them Methodists.

Wesley himself was still a seeker, and weary years passed before he found the peace of God. The real beginning of days came for him on May 24, 1738, when he went, rather reluctantly, to a little company of Christians gathered in Aldersgate Street. One of the brethren read Luther's "Preface to the Epistle to the Romans," and as he listened, he found himself strangely stirred. The Spirit of Christ, like a fragrant wind, breathed through his being. He ceased from weary, hopeless struggling, and he cast himself, as a little child, upon the arms of Jesus. Then John Wesley knew the deep, unutterable peace of God.

He at once began to preach with wholehearted conviction, expounding the great master texts of the gospel, making Christ the Alpha and Omega of every discourse. But the more earnestly he preached, the more firmly the churches were closed against him. Often, when he descended the pulpit stairs, an irate clergyman would meet him with the words, "Sir, you cannot preach here again."

John Wesley

However, the common people heard him gladly (see Mark 12:37), and gradually there gathered around him a group of men whose hearts God had touched. They formed themselves into little groups for prayer and discussion, making a chapel in Fetter Lane their headquarters. Increasing opposition drove them, with intense earnestness, to the throne of grace, and then, in the wonderful providence of God, drove them out into the fields.

In this great emancipation, George Whitefield led the way. The son of an innkeeper, he was drawn into the pleasant fellowship of the Holy Club by the influence of Charles Wesley, and when he began to preach, a great gift of eloquence was revealed in him. Soon the complaint was prevalent that he was driving people mad, and the churches began to close to him also. One day, as he declared the gospel in a building filled to the uttermost, he cast his eyes outside and saw a thousand yearning and disappointed faces. The thought seized him, *Why not go out and preach in the open?* But this was a thing unheard of. When he consulted his brethren, they condemned it as a wild idea. While thus exercised, he went to Bristol, and he preached with such fervency that within a couple weeks, every church in the place shut its doors against him in emphatic protest. There remained the prison. He preached to the poor prisoners the gospel that the church refused. But soon that door, too, was closed by order of the mayor. Thousands were hungering for the Bread of Life, but neither in church nor in prison was there room for Whitefield to dispense it. He now recognized the clear hand of God. Turning from these barred doors, he saw, far out in the fields, the beckoning hand of the Master who had found His pulpit on the green hillsides of Galilee. Whitefield obeyed.

George Whitefield

Near Bristol was a wild region known as Kingswood, once a royal preserve of land, but now a miners' country, without a church, inhabited by a rough and lawless people. Driven from Bristol, Whitefield went out to this neglected spot. On Saturday afternoon, February 17, 1739 (is it not the supreme date of that century?), he took his stand on a little green hill and began to preach the gospel. In vast amazement, about two hundred miners gathered around him. Such a sight had never been seen before. A minister, a minister in gown and neckband, preaching on a hillside! As he continued day after day, his audience soon grew to twenty thousand, who pressed upon him eagerly to hear the Word of Life. They filled the hedges. They climbed the trees. Nature itself seemed hushed to hear. A sweet summer stillness prevailed. The sun shone from a blue sky, and the strong, clear voice of the young man, eloquent with the very love of God, reached to the utmost bounds of the great assembly. Then Whitefield saw a moving sight.

He saw white channels forming in the darkened faces of the miners. The whole multitude was drenched in tears of repentance. Before he ended, the dark faces were washed white, and the dark hearts had been washed white, too! He at once wrote to John Wesley in London: "Come, the fire is kindled in the country." The summons was obeyed, and when John Wesley came and saw the grace of God, he was glad. Whitefield, called to other parts, left Wesley to continue the work, and Wesley entered upon his great career as a field preacher – that career that may be studied in his diary. From then on, the world was his parish. As he passed from place to place, the power of God followed him; yes, it travelled to the remotest parts of the country, and crossing the sea, awakened the life of the universal church.

Chapter 4

The "Wark" at Cambuslang

Cambuslang, on the outskirts of Glasgow, is now a populous and thriving town. In the eighteenth century, it was a small parish of about nine hundred souls. A memorable and far-reaching awakening took place here, and its green hills are fragrant to this day with the divine breath that breathed so sweetly there in 1742.

The work is abidingly associated with the name of William McCulloch, minister of the parish church. He was not at all a "popular" preacher. His delivery was slow and cautious, but his message was intensely biblical. He rose at five so that he could delight in the riches of divine truth. He abounded in charity, but above all, he was a man of prayer. He loved the secret place, and he was always encouraging his people to unite in praying groups and to make the main burden of their petitions the revival of God's work.

Like Elijah's servant, he eagerly scanned the heavens for the signs of coming blessing, and the news of the gracious movement under John Wesley and George Whitefield filled his soul with joy. He at once began to tell his people the story of the great revival in England and America. The church was small and in need of repair, so the services were often held in a green valley of the surrounding hills. Here, then, on Sunday evenings, after his sermon was finished, he told his flock, little by little, the great tidings that had gladdened his own heart. His preaching, more than ever, became a solemn and awakening call. For a full year he dwelt on the need of the new birth, and strictly related topics, and gradually the effect was seen in deepening reverence and a growing hunger for prayer.

God times the movements of His obedient servants with a beautiful accuracy. He now sent Whitefield to Scotland, the first of a long series of visits. In July 1741, he commenced a truly apostolic ministry in Dunfermline. When he gave out his first text, the rustle of the leaves as the whole audience opened their Bibles filled him with surprise and delight. He felt like Paul in Berea. The soil had been enriched by long and systematic study of the Scriptures, and the good seed at once took deep root. At Edinburgh he preached twice daily, and every morning he had "a levee of wounded souls." He then traveled west, and the vast graveyard of Glasgow's ancient cathedral became the birthplace of a multitude of souls. When he went south in October, Whitefield had the assurance that God had visited His people in Scotland and that greater things were in store.

In Cambuslang, the work had received a new impetus. The year of grace 1742 opened with strong hope. In January a petition was presented to Mr. McCulloch from ninety heads of families, requesting that a weekly service be held for the further ministry of the Word. Thursday was at once fixed for this purpose.

Prayer now became imperative. On Monday, February 15, and again on Tuesday and Wednesday, a group of intercessors gathered at the manse. The newly established service was held the next day, and when the sermon closed it was evident that the great power of God had been liberated. The Word, quietly delivered, cut like a sharp sword, and when the minister retired to his house, fifty people followed him in an agony of conviction. The whole night was spent by Mr. McCulloch in the blessed labor of directing these wounded souls to Christ. The following day the church doors were thrown open, and for twelve weeks he preached daily to a stricken people. The heart of their sorrow was the deep conviction that their sins had pierced the Son of God. Now the gospel was heard, as it were, for the first time, and beholding the Lamb of God, their sorrow was turned into unspeakable joy. Heaven seemed to come down to earth again, and the very glory of God seemed to shine on every hillside. A mighty hunger for the Word seized the newborn converts, and old people went to school with the children so they could learn to read the Bible. The life of the community was transformed. Drunkenness and blasphemy ceased. A spirit of tenderest love filled their hearts and shone in their eyes. Faults were confessed and forgiven. Restitution to the utmost was eagerly made. Family devotions were revived, and everyone sought to bring others to the Savior.

The tidings of this gracious movement spread far and wide, and the "Wark at Cambuslang," as it was called, became the talk of Scotland. People came flocking from all parts of the land to see the grace of God, and Mr. McCulloch now frequently ministered the Word to ten thousand people. The blessing culminated in two great Communions, the like of which Scotland had never seen before. The first was set for July 11. On the previous Tuesday, Whitefield, again in Scotland, came to Cambuslang for the first time. He preached three times – at two, at six, and at nine o'clock. The people were literally smitten down and had to be carried into the surrounding houses. When Whitefield was exhausted, Mr. McCulloch continued to preach until long past midnight. All through that night, the voice of prayer and praise was heard in the fields and barns of the country all around. On the Lord's Day, twenty thousand people assembled to hear the Word, while more than seventeen hundred pressed to the

Communion tables, sitting down by groups upon the green grass, as in Galilee of old.

So great was the blessing that it was determined to hold a second Communion on August 15. Many people traveled from afar to the sacred feast. Old Mr. Bonar, minister of Torphichen, from whom has sprung a famous and godly seed, though very frail, was determined not to miss this crowning joy. He took three days to ride the eighteen miles that lay between, and he joined Whitefield and the fine group of ministers who had come to Mr. McCulloch's assistance. More than thirty thousand hearers assembled, and three thousand sat down at the Lord's Table. The windows of heaven were again opened above the thronging multitude, and an even richer blessing was outpoured. There was indeed no room to receive it, and again the mourning of stricken hearts mingled with the song of the redeemed throughout the night.

The "wark" was of God, and it stood the test of time. When the flood of spiritual joy subsided, a rich soil remained, and a bountiful harvest was securely gathered.

Chapter 5

Brainerd and the
Indian Revival

The name of David Brainerd, like that of Robert
Murray McCheyne and Henry Martyn, lingers in
the memory of the church with a haunting sweetness.
His life was brief, but the influence of his devoted spirit
is felt to this day, moving men to a noble self-forgetting.
His place is assured in the great story of revival. John
Wesley was asked the question, "What can be done in
order to revive the work of God where it is decayed?"
John Wesley replied, "Let every preacher read carefully
over the life of David Brainerd."

David Brainerd was born in 1718 near Hartford,
Connecticut, and was orphaned at an early age. He had a
weak physical constitution, and the seeds of consumption
were early sown in his feeble frame. Throughout his life
he fought a losing battle with this terrible physical foe,

but his story is like that of James Turner of Peterhead, and shows how weakness itself, linked by faith to the power of God, can triumph gloriously.

David Brainerd

Before Brainerd entered the life of faith, he wandered long in the dreary desert of legalism. But he tells us that one day, as he walked in a thick, dark grove, unspeakable glory opened to his view. In that one moment of vision, he learned more than in all the laborious years of the past. He saw that God's will is the one fount of undefiled peace and joy. To do that will at any cost became the passion of his life.

He was trained at Yale College, and in 1742 he was licensed to preach the gospel. At first his desire had been to evangelize the heathen abroad, but his eyes were now open to the need of the poor Indians of his own land. Although they were miserably debased by the white man's vices, and despised as an inferior creation, Brainerd saw in them souls for whom Christ had died – a field ready to harvest. He eagerly accepted the appointment of the Scottish Society for Promoting Christian Knowledge to labor as their missionary among the Indians.

He had little success when he first set out. His station was at Kaunaumeek, in New York, "a most lonesome wilderness," where he lodged on a pile of straw. The Indians were indifferent or suspicious, while the white settlers bitterly resented his presence. His health began to decline rapidly, and after a year of unremitting toil and hardship, he was forced to retire from the field.

He was soon invited to the pastorate of several New England churches. The temptation to settle in East Hampton was especially great. Here, in a lovely country, amid a wealthy and kind people, he might recover his strength and spend happy and useful days.

The tender tie of a pure affection for the daughter of Jonathan Edwards also constrained him to stay. His experience at Kaunaumeek had clearly shown him that the Indian wilderness held for him certain and speedy death – and what fruit did he have to show for his labor? Surely, then, in this sweet environment, where health and love and delightful service awaited him, he should cast his lot. But as Brainerd hesitated – hesitated literally between life and death – he heard a sad cry from the far-off woods. It was the wail of "his poor Indians." No one cared for their souls! They, too, were calling him. Therefore, turning from the white church and taking his life in his hands, he set out again for the Indian wigwams. This was the decisive moment of his life. If he had settled among the good people of East Hampton, he would in all probability have regained his health and discharged a faithful ministry. However, we would never then have heard of David Brainerd.

He deliberately cut short his days, but in the brief remnant of life that remained to him, he accomplished a glorious work and unlocked a spring of heroic inspiration for generations to come. He made the uttermost sacrifice, and God gave him the uttermost reward. From this point on, his journal is the record of constant journeyings among his poor Indians, covering more than three thousand miles – through pathless forests, over dark, dangerous mountains, and in fierce rains and freezing cold. His body was reduced to a dismal state of extreme weakness. But as his strength ebbed, his compassion grew; it grew until it became a great hunger that would not be denied. He spent entire nights in agonizing prayer in the dark woods, his clothes drenched with the sweat of his travail.

Just at this point, on the very eve of revival, he felt a strange restricting. God seemed to desert him. His message began to falter. Like John Livingston at Shotts before the great outpouring, he was made to feel that he was indeed just a man, and that the blessing must come from above. When Brainerd, in complete humility, surrendered in this, all was ready for the mighty power of God to be put forth.

Suddenly – how often must that word be used in the history of revival! – suddenly, the Spirit was outpoured upon the whole region of the Susquehanna. His first audience there had consisted of four women and a few children. Now there came streaming in upon him from all sides a host of men and women who pressed upon him. Grasping the bridle of his horse, they pleaded with him with intense earnestness to tell them the way of salvation. In a great, glad wonder he looked upon them, and the text that leaped to his lips was *Herein is love* (1 John 4:10).

Men fell at his feet in anguish of soul. These were men who could bear the most intense torture without flinching – but God's arrow had now pierced them. Their pain could not be concealed, and they cried out in their distress, "Have mercy upon me." What impressed Brainerd most deeply was that although these people came to him in a multitude, each one was mourning individually. The prophecy of Zechariah was fulfilled before his eyes. The woods were filled with the sound of a great mourning, and beneath the cross, every man fell as if he and the Savior God alone were there. Gradually, as the missionary spoke, there came to them, one by one, the peace and comfort of the gospel. As the days passed, he had full proof that a heaven-sent revival had come. A passion for righteousness possessed the converts. The wretched victims of the firewater were delivered, and the Indian camps were cleansed at once from their physical and moral filthiness. The love of Christ expelled every unlovely thing. As one poor woman expressed it, "Me to be Him for all" became the motto of their lives. They became themselves ardent missionaries of the cross. The Light spread through all that dark region, and a strong Indian church was established.

Brainerd's work was done. His body, utterly exhausted by his labors, was quickly mastered by disease. But what did that matter? It had been the means of a triumphant work of faith. It endured until the divine purpose had its perfect fulfilment – and when, in 1747, in the house of Jonathan Edwards, he breathed his last, he died in an ecstasy of joy.

Chapter 6

The Great Missionary Revival

In every revival there is the reassertion of the church's missionary character. People return to Calvary, and the world is seen afresh through the eyes of Christ. The infinite compassion of Christ fills the heart, and the passion evoked by Calvary demands the whole wide world as the fruit of His sacrifice. Thus, the evangelical awakening of the eighteenth century culminated in a mighty missionary movement that restored the church's powerful witness to every nation, and established a real and growing dominion of Christ in every land.

In the accomplishment of this great work, God, who loves to uplift the small and despised, was pleased to use a poor cobbler in the Midlands of England. Wiliam Carey was born in 1761, in Paulerspury, near Northampton, and he was born again of the divine Spirit in his eighteenth year. His story is one of fierce, almost desperate, struggle with poverty. He found comfort in books, the money for which he obtained by the simple means of starving himself – so that he literally fed his mind at the expense of his body. His cobbler's shed in Hackleton became his college, and here, as he worked with open book before him, he mastered Latin, Greek, and Hebrew, and acquired a working knowledge of French and Dutch. Soon a still higher delight entered his life. He developed power as a preacher, and in 1785 he became pastor of the little Baptist church at Moulton. His salary was only 15 pounds, and he was compelled to teach a school, but this necessity that seemed to confine his usefulness was really the narrow door through which he entered upon the immeasurable field of his great lifework. It was while he taught the children geography with the aid of a leather globe he had constructed that the great missionary idea entered his mind and became the passion of his soul. Isaiah saw the Lord in the temple (Isaiah 6:1), and just as certainly did William Carey see Him in that little schoolroom. Just as certainly as Isaiah heard the voice of the Lord, William Carey heard Him say, *Whom shall I send, and who will go for us?* and just as earnestly did he respond, *Here am I, Lord, send me!* (Isaiah 6:8).

Carey was now a man of one main idea. One glorious thought dominated his whole life. Christ had died for all mankind, and the glad tidings of salvation must be carried to every creature under heaven. In conversation, this was his uppermost, ever-recurring theme, but he found no response. The missionary enterprise seemed wholly utopian – "a wild, impracticable scheme." Repulsed by his brethren, he turned to the printing press. He wrote his *Inquiry*,[2] showing the still-binding force of Christ's last command, and pleading for united prayer for people and resources. Repression only served to make the fire within him burn more intensely, and gradually some of the men around him began to share his passion – notably Andrew Fuller of Kettering. Then, after six years of waiting, his great opportunity came. Now pastor of the church in Harvey Lane, Leicester, he was invited to preach to the ministers' meeting at Nottingham, and in his sermon, the long-curbed fire leaped forth, a fire that was destined to set the whole church ablaze. He took for his text Isaiah 54:2-3, apply-ing its truth in two mighty expressions that have been the inspiration of missionary endeavor from that day to this: "Expect great things from God. Attempt great things for God."

His brethren were deeply stirred, but even then there was danger that feeling might evaporate in tears and would fail to move the springs of action. The meeting ended and the ministers were about to separate. Even Andrew Fuller, on whom he had counted, made no sign.

---

2   The title of William Carey's book was *An Enquiry Into the Obligations of Christians, to Use Means for the Conversion of the Heathens In Which the Religious State of the Different Nations of the World, the Success of Former Undertakings, and the Practicability of Further Undertakings, Are Considered.*

It was a moment big with fate. If it passed without some definite deed, all was lost. In an agony, he seized the arm of Fuller and cried, "Oh, are you, after all, going to do nothing?" Fuller looked into Carey's eyes and found their appeal irresistible. He recalled his brethren, and then there was inserted in their minutes this momentous decision: "That a place be prepared against the next meeting at Kettering for forming a Baptist Society for propagating the Gospel among the heathen." The Society was formed a few months later, on October 2, 1792 (it is one of God's dates), in the low-roofed back parlor of Widow Wallis, at Kettering. It consisted in the beginning of twelve men, and its first subscriptions amounted to £13 2s. 6d. Its first secretary was Andrew Fuller, and its first missionary was William Carey.

The Society was nearly strangled in its birth. The East India Company refused to transport missionaries to India. It considered them more dangerous than the pestilence. Thus Carey and his companion, Dr. Thomas, sailed in a Danish vessel, and it was finally in the Danish soil of Serampore that the young Society struck its roots. Long and cruel were the hardships he endured, but he toiled and toiled with unfailing faith and hope. He labored for seven years without a convert. Then Krishna Pal, long burdened by the sense of sin, found in Carey's Savior the great Rest-Giver and the great Deliverer. Carey baptized him in the river on December 28, 1800, the first of a countless host who, from every kindred and tongue and nation, have come to adore the Name that is above every name.

William Carey

For fourteen months, no news came to England of the great venture of faith, but Fuller and his little Society labored in prayer and held fast the ropes in the homeland, assured that God was with the workers in the dark mine beneath. When at last Carey's letters arrived, a joy that was truly unspeakable and full of glory filled their hearts. They came together and sang the hymn of William Williams of Pantycelyn, the triumph song of missions:

> O'er those gloomy hills of darkness,
> Look, my soul, be still and gaze;
> All the promises do travail
> With a glorious day of grace.

In that same year of 1794, they began to publish their "Periodical Accounts" relating the story of the mission, and then fast-crowding and glorious events showed that the Spirit of missions had indeed gone forth. These simple pages went through the land and over the earth, and society after society sprang into being in England, Scotland, Ireland, Germany, France, the Netherlands, and America. In 1794 the London Missionary Society, and in 1799 the Church Missionary Society, entered upon their glorious careers. So deeply moved was Robert Haldane that he at once sold his estate of Airthrey and gave himself and all he had to the heavenly cause. Thwarted by the government in his plan of going abroad, his eyes were opened to see that the great field of missions is one field, and that it begins at a person's own door. He and his brother James became missionaries in Scotland, and they carried the gospel to the remotest glens of their native land. Haldane's Home Mission, now merged in the Baptist Union of Scotland, is one of the finest proofs of the great law enunciated by Dr. Chalmers – that foreign missions act upon the home church, not by exhaustion, but by fermentation, revitalizing its drooping life. On the other hand, the manna that is kept unused becomes a fount of corruption. When the life energies of a church are restrained and turned in selfishly upon itself, they immediately begin to break it up; they are transmuted into the dreadful and horrible activities of death. However, the church lives and flourishes exceedingly when it gives its life to a perishing world.

William Carey never returned to his homeland, but lived to a ripe old age in India, dying in 1834, no fewer than thirty-four distinct translations of the Bible into the Indian tongues having come from his hands. On his tombstone, by his own desire, are inscribed these words: "A wretched, poor, and helpless worm, on Thy kind arms I fall."

Chapter 7

Robert Haldane in Geneva

Geneva is forever associated with the great name of John Calvin, whose massive theology is not unlike the majestic Alps that tower above the city. But in the days of Robert Haldane, Geneva had long discarded the faith of her fathers, and a deep darkness shrouded the once radiant fount of Protestant truth. Infidel philosophers such as Edward Gibbon and Voltaire found a friendly home in her neighborhood. Her noble school of theology was corrupted by an insidious Unitarianism. The Bible was entirely set aside as a textbook. Plato and Seneca took the place of Christ and Paul. During the whole four years' course, the only use made of the sacred volume was in the teaching of Hebrew, when a few Psalms and chapters were read. The students were thus profoundly ignorant of gospel truth, and willingly consumed the new theology of that day, which magnified the natural goodness of man and denied our Lord's divinity.

In 1816 Robert Haldane was strongly moved to visit the Continent. His eyes had been gladdened by a work of grace in his own land, and he longed to see the light spreading to the still darkened lands of Europe. The peace had opened doors long closed, and at the end of the year he set out, accompanied by his like-minded wife. He expected to be gone for six weeks, but three years, the three greatest years of his life, were to elapse before he returned. In Paris he found a spiritual gloom that could be felt, and it was no wonder, for not long before his visit, a diligent search had been made, and not a single copy of the Scriptures could be found in all the capital! Here he sought in vain an opening for the gospel, and then he went on to Geneva. As he passed through its ancient gates, he prayed fervently for divine leading, for he did not know one person there. At first all things seemed unfavorable. Day after day he labored to find a door of utterance, and he was on the point of departure when suddenly the whole situation changed.

How often has it been found that what we call a trivial incident is really a finely formed link in the golden chain of Providence! An old pastor had promised to conduct a short excursion beyond the walls, but prevented by sickness, he sent in his place a young man, a student of divinity. Mr. Haldane at once began to speak of the gospel, and to his great joy, as the youth listened, his wonder awoke. He returned with Mr. Haldane to his chambers, and continued with him until late at night, hearing remarkable things. The next morning he appeared with another student who was equally curious. So astonished were these young men by what they heard that they could speak of nothing else to their fellows. A very strange teacher had come to Geneva, they said, a man of one book, and this book, the Bible, was indeed a great book that was well worth the perusal of divinity students! They had been amazed to find that problems that perplexed them were solved in a moment by some passage from this wonderful volume, for the man who made so much of it was a "living concordance" and could at once turn to the very text that was needed! "He knew the Bible like Calvin!" These reports so stirred up the interest of the others that soon Mr. Haldane was besieged by inquirers, and it was in the attempt to satisfy these seekers that his famous Home Bible College, as it might be called, came into being.

It was arranged for about thirty students to meet with him three times a week and spend two evening hours, from six to eight, in the study of the Holy Scriptures. They were seated around a long table on which were placed copies of the Bible in French, German, English, and other languages, besides the original Hebrew and Greek. Mr. Haldane's method was simplicity itself. At first they were full of questions and every difficulty, and every misunderstanding was at once brought to the test of Scripture. He spent no time in argument, but opening his well-worn Bible, pointed to some pertinent text, saying, "Look here – how do you understand this? What do you think?" As he did so, light would dart from the Book and difficulties would vanish like ice in the burning sun.

Having thus cleared the ground, he proceeded to sow the divine seed. He began a systematic study of the Epistle to the Romans. Here they were at once confronted with a terrible truth that flatly contradicted their accepted teaching – the truth of man's depravity, his helplessness, and his utter sinfulness. Gathering all the force of Scripture on this great fundamental point, he earnestly pressed home the truth until the awakened conscience gave full assent to it. Then what he had hoped and prayed for came to pass. A very beautiful thing happened. The merely intellectual thirst for knowledge changed into a deep spiritual concern. The theological class became a class of anxious inquirers! How eagerly now did they follow the exposition of the great epistle as their teacher passed on to the grand disclosure of the grace of God in the gospel!

It was the great hour of Haldane's life, and he knew it! He knew the value of a student won for Christ. He saw not only these young men before him, but he also saw the thousands who would come under their influence. If he could only bring these men to Christ, this upper room in Geneva might be the spring of biblical revival flowing to Europe. A deep solemnity came into his speech. The young men felt, as they listened, that a prophet charged with a great mission was among them. And to the praise of the God of all grace and to his own unspeakable joy, he succeeded. One by one, sitting around that table before the open Book, they surrendered to Jesus Christ! When Haldane passed on to the great chapters on sanctification and the Christian life, his class had become a group of men whose hearts God had touched.

Such a remarkable work could not be accomplished without stirring up the wrath of the professors and clergy of Geneva. A bitter persecution followed, but God preserved the precious life He had created in a wonderful way. When Haldane moved on to Montauban to win further victories for the gospel, God sent another teacher to continue the work. Henry Drummond (well named!), a talented and wealthy young Englishman and a devoted servant of Jesus Christ, was on a voyage to the Holy Land when a heaven-sent storm forced his ship to seek refuge in the port of Genoa. Here he heard of the Student Revival, changed his plans, and came on to Geneva, arriving just two days before Mr. Haldane's departure.

The persecution itself was made the instrument of a larger blessing. It ultimately scattered the students throughout Europe, and thus realized Haldane's original intention. Henry Pyt became the missionary of the Bearn and the Pyrenees. Merle d'Aubigne, driven from his native city, went to Berlin and became a notable preacher and the famous historian of the Reformation. Dr. Gaussen, the author of *Theopneustia*, and Dr. Caesar Malan exercised large influence in our own and other lands. Charles Rieu went to Denmark, where he finished his course after a brief but fruitful ministry. Felix Neff, the "Apostle of the High Alps," though not a student of Haldane, traced his inspiration to the same source. Christopher Burckhardt died at Aleppo. These are but a few of the noble names in that honored group. In later days it was found that the seeds of many rich harvests were sown in that sacred upper room in Geneva. In the town itself, a living church arose, and Geneva became again as in Calvin's day – the fount of evangelical truth.

Chapter 8

The Kilsyth Revival

The spiritual awakening that has made Kilsyth memorable in the records of grace is naturally associated with the name of William Chalmers Burns, its most honored instrument, but there was a long, patient preparation in the faithful ministry of his father. When W. H. Burns began his work there as parish minister in 1821, the population of the town was about three thousand, for the most part consisting of miners and weavers. Its morality was very low. Drunkenness and its kindred vices were rampant. All bargains and payments were made over the "friendly glass." The session clerk had his office in the tavern, where he soon became a victim of the prevailing sin, while the typical funeral service was composed of long prayers interspersed with rounds of drinking.

One of Mr. Burns' first acts was to found a temperance society, but his primary and abiding hope was in the revival of God's work. He stirred and quickened the embers of a prayer meeting that had sprung from the Cambuslang Revival of 1742. This meeting can be traced through a hundred years, connecting the movements in Cambuslang and Kilsyth, and suggests the fact that revivals that seem so sporadic are really closely and vitally related. One of the most precious fruits of a true revival is the establishment of a living prayer meeting, and it is here also that we find the seed of revival.

As the years went on, the need of a divine awakening burdened the pastor's heart increasingly, and more and more his ministry was directed to this great and glorious end. He eagerly studied the story of revivals, and in 1822 we find him with Dr. George Wright of Stirling bending over the old records of the kirk (church) session, reading of wonders of grace in 1742, and fervently praying that the glory of God might again be revealed. In those distant days, God had greatly used a very devoted pastor of the church, the Rev. James Robb, and that he might impress afresh the lessons of that fruitful ministry, Mr. Burns took his stand one Sunday afternoon upon the grave of his honored predecessor and preached earnestly to his people. Gradually it became evident that rich blessing was yet in store for Kilsyth. There was a deepened seriousness in public worship. The prayer meeting was packed. Gracious drops, the forerunners of the coming shower, began to fall. There were some undoubted conversions, and faith grew strong.

In 1839 the full blessing was outpoured. In His sovereign grace, God was pleased to use the minister's son as His fitting instrument. William C. Burns had been laboring in Dundee, in the church of the saintly Robert Murray McCheyne, and he had deeply felt the fragrance of that beautiful spirit. There he had seen a genuine work of grace, and there God had been preparing him. One touch only was needed to make him a polished shaft in the divine hand – the touch of sorrow. It was given through the death of a dear relative, and as the young man stood by the grave of his brother-in-law in Paisley, the shadow of death was the shadow of God's hand, laying firm hold of His servant. On his return home, a very manifest unction accompanied his preaching. He spoke with power at Banton on Saturday, and again on Sunday.

On Tuesday, July 23, the great refreshing came. On that day, a large assembly gathered to hear him in the marketplace of Kilsyth. Rain began to fall, and they entered the church, which was soon filled to overflowing. Stairs, hallways, and the porch were blocked by eager people.

Solemn prayer was followed by the reading of the second chapter of Acts, and then, taking for his text Psalm 110:3, *Thy people shall be willing in the day of thy power*, the young man began to address the people. As he spoke, a wonderfully sweet and tender spirit came upon the gathering. Hearts melted and tears began to flow. At the close, he told the story of the Shotts Revival in 1630 – how John Livingston, himself a native of Kilsyth, in preparation for an after-communion service, spent a whole night in prayer; how God gave him such a vision of His glory and his own unworthiness that he turned to flee; how his friends found him in the fields and gently forced him to return; how the trembling youth stood up to speak and was suddenly clothed with irresistible power so that on the spot five hundred people, from all ranks of society, were converted through that one sermon.

As William Burns recounted this marvelous work of God, he saw that the same Spirit was moving the people before him. An intense earnestness seized him, and he urged the people there and then to accept Christ, clinching his message with the solemn words, "No cross, no crown." As he uttered those words, the whole audience broke down and an indescribable scene followed. The arrows of conviction smote the people, and from every part of the building there was a cry of agony: "What must I do to be saved?"

Happily, there was a group of prepared servants of God ready for such an emergency. The stricken ones were gathered in the vestry and session house, and were dealt with individually. Many soon obtained the peace of God, but others remained under painful conviction for days. The church was opened for daily services, and night after night for months, a great reaping took place. In the marketplace and in the churchyard, assemblies of three or four thousand were addressed by Mr. Burns. A great hunger for prayer and for the Word of God possessed the people. They could not be satisfied! The effect upon the community was very great. It was largely transformed. Alcohol received a fatal blow. The town was cleansed from its vice. Loom shops became places of prayer, and many a home became a Bethel. It proved to be an abiding work. The converts went on from strength to strength, and the very memory of the revival has remained a blessed influence in the place to this day.

Chapter 9

The Revival in Dundee

After ten months' labor in Larbert and Dunipace, Robert McCheyne was called to Dundee, and here in the parish of St. Peter's he found his great lifework. He was appalled at first by its heathenism. He mourned its "idolatry and hardness of heart" and the feeble influence of the surviving church, but with fortitude of faith, he set himself to his task. Very soon he established a weekly prayer meeting on Thursday evenings, and here he read to his people or told them the story of God's marvelous work in past revivals. Once again, as so often before and since, the seed of the great harvest was sown in the prayer meeting.

He devoted himself to his pastoral duties, and often, after several hours of visitation, he would again meet the gathered families under some friendly roof and declare the Word of Life. Preaching was to him an unceasing delight. It was the unfolding of the beauty and glory of Him whom he loved. He carefully prepared his message. One of his oft-quoted sayings is: "Beaten oil – beaten oil for the lamps of the sanctuary." Like John Bunyan, he was always in the Word. He was asked one day if he was ever afraid of running short of sermons, and he replied, "No; I am just an interpreter of Scripture in my sermons, and when the Bible runs dry, then I shall."

He loved to make his appeals to the careless "on the back of some solid truth." God's Word was in his hands like a hammer, yet no one ever preached with greater sweetness and tenderness.

But McCheyne was himself his greatest sermon, and this is the secret of his success. He walked with God in the beauty of holiness. Our Lord's presence seemed to surround him, diffusing a heavenly aroma. His very manner, his bearing as of a man standing in God's presence, was often the means of awakening indifferent sinners, so that people who could not remember a word he said found themselves with an unforgettable impression that God had drawn very near to them.

From the beginning, God set His seal to his ministry. Callers of an unusual type appeared at the manse – men and women in trembling anxiety of soul! Like the physician's house during an epidemic, his home was marked and became the resort of sin-sick souls. People gathered from all parts of the town and district to his ministry. That surest sign of coming revival – a growing prayer meeting – was now appearing, when a strange thing happened.

Robert McCheyne

This instrument of revival, so delicately fashioned and so perfectly adapted, was suddenly, in the eyes of men, laid aside by the great Master Builder, and another uplifted. Never robust, and unsparing in his labors, McCheyne broke down under the strain of his strenuous pastorate. Serious heart trouble developed, and he was compelled to leave the scene of his delightful duties and seek rest and renewal, first in Edinburgh, and later in a pilgrimage of inquiry among the Jews in the Holy Land.

It may be that people were regarding the instrument too fondly and were forgetting the hand of Sovereign Grace that wielded it. But McCheyne was not really set aside. God had used his preaching most noticeably, and now He would use his prayer! During all this period of isolation, his heart bore the burden of Dundee, and like Epaphras, he labored fervently in prayers (Colossians 4:12). Severe sickness again fell upon him in the East, and he lay at the gates of death. But still he agonized for his flock, and it was one day, while thus he travailed on the brink of eternity in far-off Bouja, near Smyrna, that the great shower began to fall in Dundee.

William C. Burns, already used so mightily in the Kilsyth Revival, was further honored in opening the floodgate of blessing in Dundee. He took McCheyne's place during his absence, and it was on a visit to Kilsyth that the memorable awakening took place there, on July 23, 1839. On his return to Dundee at the Thursday evening prayer meeting on August 10, Burns spoke of the wonders he had just witnessed, and invited those to remain "who felt the need of an outpouring of the Spirit to convert them." About a hundred people waited, and as he addressed them, suddenly that infinitely tender Spirit, whose incoming in power can never be mistaken, came upon the people, and the whole assembly was bathed in tears. From that night the work went on increasing in might. The church was opened and was densely crowded night after night for four months. The Word of God proclaimed by Mr. Burns and like-minded ministers had a piercing effect. The most tender presentation of Christ produced the bitterest agony of soul so that strong men cried out for mercy in the midst of the congregation.

The whole city was moved, for Christ again was centered amid an adoring people. Whole families were affected at once, and were found mourning apart as in the prediction of Zechariah (Zechariah 12:12). A great spirit of reverence came upon the community, and sin was greatly restrained.

Renewed in strength, Mr. McCheyne returned to his flock while the showers were still falling. No slightest tinge of jealousy disturbed his fellowship with Mr. Burns. Each had learned great humility at the Master's feet, and they cooperated in pure disinterested love. He has described his first service after his return – the church crowded to the doors, the pulpit stairs filled on one side with the aged, and on the other side with little children; the wonderful singing, so sweet, so tender and affecting; the intense hearing of the Word and the manifest hunger for the Bread of Life; and then the strange trip homeward, when the people crowded around him in the street, pressing upon him, as upon his Master in Galilee, constraining him to stop and pray and speak again, and yet again on his way to the manse!

During these days of heaven upon earth, a multitude passed from death to life. They were very largely from among the poor and working classes. He laments that the rich were almost untroubled. Then gradually the flood subsided and flowed quietly on, a brimming river within its banks. The work stood, for it was maintained by unceasing prayer. For a time, no fewer than thirty-nine prayer meetings were held weekly in connection with his church, and five of these were carried on entirely by children. McCheyne loved the children dearly, and had himself the free joyousness of an innocent child. The work among these little ones was remarkably deep and abiding, as is witnessed by his tract "Another Lily Gathered." These lambs of the flock were lovingly welcomed, and at the Lord's Table their bright young faces, radiant with heavenly joy, gave a fresh sweetness to the feast of love.

Robert McCheyne had now three years to live. He was haunted by the conviction that his career would be short. During those last years, a deep solemnity and a great yearning love marked his utterance. He truly preached as a dying man to dying men, watching for their souls as one who must soon give an account. The sense of a fast approaching end saved him from the snare of popularity. "Oh, for closest communion with God," he cried, "until soul and body – head, face, and heart – shine with divine brilliancy! But oh, for a holy ignorance of our shining!"

His labors increased and extended, and the memory of his evangelistic tours lingers in many parts of Scotland to this day. The end came on March 25, 1843. The typhus fever, raging in his parish, suddenly seized his weak frame, and after a very brief illness, he succumbed. In his delirium he was always in spirit with his beloved flock – praying, preaching, and directing them heavenward. He died with his hand uplifted in the act of benediction.

After his death, a letter was opened that was addressed to him by someone who had heard his last sermon. The letter said:

I hope you will pardon a stranger for addressing to you a few lines. I heard you preach last Sunday evening, and it pleased God to bless that sermon to my soul. It was not so much what you said as your manner of speaking that struck me. I saw in you a beauty of holiness that I never saw before. You also said something in your prayer that struck me very much. It was, "You know that we love You." Oh, sir, what would I give that I might say to my blessed Savior: "You know that I love You."

Chapter 10

The American Awakening

In Britain we speak of the 1859 revival, but in America of the 1858 revival, for the gracious movement of that year was remarkable in its universality, purity, and rich fruitfulness. A growing corruption marked the years that preceded it. The gulf between rich and poor was widened by an extraordinary luxury. Crimes of violence rapidly increased. Spiritualism, in its modern phase, had its rise in America about this time, and soon its foul flood was flowing strongly. It fiercely assailed the marriage relation, and it openly espoused the doctrines of "free love." Corruption was open and unashamed in commercial and political life, while the cruel evil of slavery was still established by the law of the land. Atheism lifted its head boldly, and the majority of people seemed thrice hardened in indifference.

By the terrible onset of evil, the American church was driven to God. Early in 1856, Christians began to pray plainly for revival. The denominations drew together. The church united its forces at the throne of grace. A great commercial crisis at the end of 1857 was undoubtedly used by the divine Spirit to deepen the sense of need. Banks stopped payment every week. Failures were numbered by thousands. In a severe winter, tens of thousands of the unemployed wandered about the streets, a pathetic and heart-moving spectacle. In this year, a gathering of two hundred ministers was held in Pittsburgh, and after fervent prayer, an address was issued to be read in the various churches on January 1, 1858, recommending practical measures for the revival of true religion, such as definite preaching on the subject, and house-to-house visitation.

But the greatest measure, and that which was preeminently blessed, was united prayer. Indeed, the revival of 1858 should be known as "The Revival of the United Prayer Meeting," for this was not only the fount of the great blessing, but it was throughout its course the primary, and almost sole, instrument of the divine Spirit.

In general, some great name is associated with a revival. One man is particularly used. But the movement of 1858 is exceptional. It is not linked with any outstanding personality. It is thus difficult to establish a place of origin. The wonderful fact is this: in answer to the church's united cry, ascending from all parts of the land, the Spirit of God, in a very quiet way, and suddenly, throughout the whole extent of the United States, renewed the church's life and awakened in the community around it a great thirst for God. Thus it came about that in the same city, the movement began at the same time in different quarters and proceeded for a while before the fact became generally known. As in the miracle of 2 Kings 3, into the thirsty valley that was filled with ditches by the labor of believing, praying men, there came suddenly the quiet flow of the gracious Spirit, and in a moment the churches became channels brimming with the living water. When the American church awoke to the full consciousness of the miracle, it found that from east to west and from north to south, the whole land was alive with daily prayer meetings, and it was in these daily united prayer meetings that the great majority of the conversions took place.

Two of these meetings are noteworthy. Jeremiah Lanphier, longing intensely for revival, begged a few of his fellow Christians to meet with him. For some time he was alone in the appointed place of prayer on September 23, 1857. Later in the day he was joined by five others. This was the origin of the famous Fulton Street Noon Prayer Meeting in New York, which still continues as of the day of this writing. When the blessing came, this meeting at once increased mightily in numbers and power.

In Jayne's Hall, four thousand met daily to wait upon God. Drawn from every class, they were gathered together in a great stillness, broken only for a while by the sobs of the repentant. Then brief, earnest prayers would be offered – often only a few broken sentences. The presence of God, vividly realized, produced a marvelous quietude and orderliness. Brief exhortations, or the repetition of a single text, pierced the heart like a knife. At the end of the hour, the multitude quietly dispersed and returned to business, but they looked as Jacob looked when the sun rose upon Penuel.

This took place everywhere throughout the land, and day by day many were drawn gently into the body of Christ. Joyous song and fullhearted confession marked the movement. "Stand up for Jesus," the dying words of a young minister, suddenly taken in the midst of great service, became the great watchword of the revival.

The divine revival appeared in the most unlikely places. A large number of the elderly were gathered in. White-haired penitents knelt with little children at the throne of grace. Whole families of Jews were brought to their Messiah. Deaf-mutes were reached by the glad tidings, and although their tongues were still, their faces so shone that they became effective messengers of the gospel. The most hardened atheists and unbelievers were melted, some being led to Christ by the hand of a little child.

Nor was the blessing confined to the land. The Spirit of God moved upon the face of the waters, and a multitude of sailors saw a great light. It was as if a vast cloud of blessing hovered over land and sea. As ships drew near the American ports, they came within a definite zone of heavenly influence. Ship after ship arrived with the same tale of sudden conviction and conversion. It was wonderful beyond words! On one ship, a captain and the entire crew of thirty men found Christ out at sea and entered the harbor rejoicing.

Perhaps the most remarkable awakening took place on a battleship. The *North Carolina* lay in the harbor of New York. The ship held about a thousand men. Among these were four Christians who discovered their spiritual kinship and agreed to meet for prayer. They were permitted to use a very secluded part of the ship on the lowest deck, far below the water line. Here, then, they gathered one evening. They were only four men, but they were a united group. The great prerequisite of the revival was here, for they represented three denominations. One was an Episcopalian, another was a Presbyterian, and the other two were Baptists. As they knelt in the dim light of a tiny lamp, the Spirit of God suddenly filled their hearts with such a joy of salvation that they burst into song. The strange, sweet strain rose to the decks above and created a great astonishment there.

Their ungodly shipmates came running down. They came to mock, but the mighty power of God had been liberated by rejoicing faith. It gripped them, and in one moment their derisive laugh was changed into the cry of repentant sinners! Large fellows, giants in stature, and many of them giants in sin, were literally smitten down and knelt humbly beside the four praying men like little children. A most gracious work immediately began in the depths of the great ship. The prayer meeting was held night after night, and conversions took place daily. Soon they had to send ashore for help, and ministers joyfully came out to assist. A large number were added to the various churches, and the battleship became a veritable house of God! The *North Carolina* was a receiving ship, from which men were constantly drafted to other ships. The converts of the revival were thus scattered throughout the navy. A revival convert is a burning brand. The Word of the Lord spread rapidly from ship to ship. Wherever they were, they started a prayer meeting and became a soul-winning group. Thus ship after ship left the harbor of New York for foreign seas, each carrying its group of rejoicing converts, and the Word of God was carried to the ends of the earth.

> *Great and marvellous are thy works, Lord God Almighty* (Revelation 15:3).

Chapter 11

The Ulster Revival of 1859

In 1855, Rev. J. H. Moore, pastor of the Presbyterian church in Connor, urged one of his young men to do "something more" for God. "Could you not gather at least six of your unsaved neighbors and spend an hour with them in reading and searching the Word of God?" The young man agreed to attempt "something more," and the result was the beginning of the Tannybrake Sunday school. After two years' labor, the teachers of this little school again did "something more." They asked the parents of the children to come to a meeting for prayer and Bible reading after Sunday school ended. Only one responded at first, but the meeting grew, and soon the Sunday school teachers' prayer meeting became intensely engaging, for the Spirit of God came pouring into this newly opened channel. "Christ and the cross" became the one absorbing theme of the gathering, and an intense desire to win souls for Christ seized the workers.

Among these praying people were four young men – McQuilken, Meneely, Wallace, and Carlisle – who were very strongly bound together in the fellowship of prayer. The story of George Muller awakened within them a mighty faith in God as the hearer of prayer. They began to meet regularly in the old schoolhouse of Kells, pouring out their hearts in passionate supplication for revival. Like-minded brethren joined them, and now obvious conversions, clearly following definite and insistent prayer, greatly encouraged them. In 1858 came the news of the American awakening. They heard how twelve thousand businessmen in New York met daily for prayer, and like Jacob (Genesis 32:26), they cried, "We will not let You go, except You bless us." Nor was the answer delayed. Prayer meetings multiplied all around them. Daily conversions took place.

A great revival is like a forest fire. You may trace its early course, following the first thin line of flame, but soon its progress is so swift and widely diffused that the eye can no longer keep pace with it. The flame bursts forth at once in many places, and now we see only one great conflagration. So it was with this marvelous work of grace. You might observe its course in Connor and a little beyond in 1858, but in 1859 the heavenly fire was leaping up and spreading in all directions through Antrim, Down, Derry, Tyrone, and the other counties of Ulster, and to this day 1859 is remembered as the preeminent year of grace.

As it advanced, it burned with a fiercer intensity. In Connor the conversions were of a comparatively quiet type, but in Ahoghill, Ballymena, and elsewhere there was a great smiting down. Sin was felt as a crushing and intolerable burden, and men and women often fell to the earth and continued for days in a state of utter prostration. Others were suddenly pierced as by a sharp sword, and their agonized cry for help was heard in the streets and in the fields. For example, a farmer is returning from the market in Ballymena. His mind is wholly intent upon the day's bargain. He pauses, takes out some money, and begins to count it. Suddenly a sublime Presence envelops him. In a moment, his only thought is that he is a sinner standing on the brink of hell. His silver is scattered, and he falls upon the dust of the highway, crying out for mercy.

There was a wonderful work among the children. The blessing had come to Coleraine, and one day the schoolmaster observed a boy so troubled that he was quite unfit for lessons. He graciously sent the boy home in the company of an older boy who had already found peace. As the two lads went on their way, they saw an empty house, and they went into it for prayer. While they knelt, the painful burden lifted from the boy's heart. He sprang to his feet in a transport of joy. Returning to the school, he ran up to the teacher and, with a beaming face, cried out, "Oh, I am so happy! I have the Lord Jesus in my heart." The effect of these simple words was very great. Boy after boy rose and silently slipped from the room. In a little while the master followed and discovered his boys stretched alongside the wall of the playground, every one apart and on his knees! Very soon their silent prayer became a bitter cry. It was heard by those within and pierced their hearts. They cast themselves upon their knees, and their cry for mercy was heard in the girls' schoolroom above. In a few moments the whole school was upon its knees, and its wail of distress was heard in the street outside. Neighbors and those who were passing by came flocking in, and all, as they crossed the threshold, came under the same convicting power. Every room was filled with men, women, and children seeking the Lord. The ministers of the town and men of prayer were sent for, and the whole day was spent in directing these mourners to the Lord Jesus. That school proved to be for many the house of God and the very gate of heaven.

It pleased God to use, in a very remarkable manner, the simple testimony of the four young men of Connor. Through them the revival reached the capital. Suddenly, ministers who had toiled in vain for years found themselves surrounded by sin-sick souls clamoring for the life-giving Word. If it had not been for the loving cooperation of Sunday school teachers and other friends, they would quickly have been exhausted with the work. Vast and memorable gatherings were held. Districts that had been notorious as the scenes of party strife witnessed the triumph of the gospel of peace. Bitter opponents knelt together at the Savior's feet. Belfast became like a city of God.

Chapter 12

The Aberdeenshire Revival of 1859

I n 1859, the heavenly rain cloud that so mightily refreshed the American church in the previous year crossed the Atlantic, outpoured upon Ulster an unspeakable blessing, and then hovered over the whole extent of the British Isles. Nowhere was the outpouring more marvelous than in Aberdeenshire. For some years before, many people had mourned in secret the long spiritual dearth, and as God's set time approached, these people gathered into little praying groups throughout the county. In Aberdeen itself, there were quite a few of these watchful groups of intercessors, the largest of which met on Saturday evenings in the Free North Church.

It was surely in answer to these prayers that Reginald Radcliffe, a Liverpool lawyer, came to Aberdeen at the end of 1858. He came to conduct a ten days' mission. It extended to five months. In the most unpretentious manner, he began in the small mission hall of Albion Street Congregational Church. Here he was content to labor first among the boys and girls, but soon men and women came to hear his simple and earnest appeals. His message breathed the love of God in its infinite tenderness, but was full of terrible warning to those who rejected Christ, calling constantly for instant decision. Soon old Greyfriars' Parish Church was opened to him, and the work then grew with great rapidity until the whole city was deeply moved. He frequently preached six or seven times on Sundays, and so great was the hunger for the Word that whenever a congregation dispersed, the waiting multitude outside at once poured in and again filled the place.

It became known that in the house of Mr. Brand, in Dee Place, anxious inquirers would be welcomed. Many people flocked to this house at the close of the services, and every room was filled with weeping penitents. Memorable meetings were held on the Broadhill and on the links by the seashore, and here Duncan Matheson, with George Campbell, James Smith, Dr. Duncan, and other zealous ministers of the city, cooperated with Mr. Radcliffe. For a time divine things formed the one absorbing theme of conversation. People could be seen reading the Bible in the railway carriages and in the streets, and even customers in the shops, when they had completed their purchases, would make eager inquiries as to the way of salvation.

Ducan Matheson

A passion for prayer and for the Word of God seized the converts. They spent many hours together in prayerful study, and all-night prayer meetings were held in Rubislaw Quarries. As in every revival, these praying converts became most powerful evangelists, their abundant life overflowing in soul-winning service. Organized by Mr. Radcliffe, in whom the gift of wise leadership was fully consecrated, they went forth to the surrounding districts, and Aberdeen became a fount of spiritual life to the whole county.

In the little town of Old Meldrum, Radcliffe's faith was tested in a very remarkable manner. The Free Church was crowded to hear him. Expecting an address of extraordinary eloquence, the people were greatly disappointed by the simple, unadorned message of the evangelist. At the end of the service, the workers gathered around him in dismay. Not one person had remained in response to his appeal. But now the God of wonders revealed Himself through the man who completely trusted Him. "Friends," said Radcliffe, "have faith in God. Let us ask God to send them back."

Then he prayed, speaking to God with the simplicity of a child addressing his father. As he continued in prayer, there was a movement at the door. Someone entered, then another and another. The people were all coming back! On their way homeward, even as they were criticizing "the poor discourse" they had just heard, a divine hand stopped them and compelled them to return! All cold indifference was now gone. The simplest word pierced and melted their hearts. Soon the whole assembly – children, youths and maidens, fathers and mothers – were bathed in tears at the feet of Jesus. Old Mr. Garioch, the minister of the church, was delighted. His face shone like an angel's, and that night a work of grace began that continued for months and entirely transformed the community.

If there were space, one would gladly tell the story of James Turner, the Peterhead cooper, who continued Radcliffe's work. He was devoid of learning and had no gift of utterance. He was afflicted with the disease of consumption, and when his great work began, he was a dying consumptive whose days were nearly numbered.

James Turner

He was little in stature, his voice was feeble, and his eye was deformed by a squint. However, this frail, broken, disfigured vessel was filled with a passionate love for Jesus Christ, an intense hungering compassion for souls, and an invincible faith in God. He could pray! Therefore, God was able to lift him up. Out of weakness, God made him strong, and in two crowded years of glorious life, He used the dying consumptive man to win eight thousand souls for Him!

On December 6, in the little fishing village of St. Combs, he began his memorable mission. He went from village to village, and everywhere along the seacoast his course was marked by a trail of the divine revival. As he went on, the blessing increased, and his coming was awaited with intense eagerness. Then, as happens when revival reaches its flood tide, a wave of great joy passed over the people. They crowded around him and marched together from town to town, singing as only they can sing who have drunk "the royal wine of heaven,"[3] the *joy unspeakable and full of glory* (1 Peter 1:8). In this way he at last reached Banff, and the night of March 10 is one much to be remembered by the church there. It was found impossible to dismiss the people, and through the whole night a great reaping went on. Many of the most notorious sinners in the town were saved, and many who first saw the Lord

---

3   "The royal wine of heaven" is a phrase from a hymn by Horatius Bonar (1808-1889) that begins with "Here, gracious Lord, we see You face to face."

that night went forth to declare His glory in all parts of the earth. Turner had much of the spirit of McCheyne, and his end was like his. The matchless love of Christ filled his vision, and his last words were "Christ is all."

Time tested the Aberdeenshire revival and proved that it had the enduring quality of its native granite. Fifty years later, at a jubilee celebration meeting in 1910, a multitude gave thanks to God for its precious and abiding fruits, manifest not only in the county itself, but in every part of the world. The material results alone have captured the careless eye. A gentleman once drew his friend's attention to several rows of beautiful cottages and said:

Look! These houses have sprung up as if by magic in place of the wretched hovels in which the fisher folk used to live. Formerly the money that came from the deep salt sea went down into the depths of that more dark and bitter sea, the tavern. All that is changed. The revival came. The tavern was dried up to the bottom, and you see the hard-won earnings of the fishermen in these quality and comfortable homes. Revival is a reality here. You can see it, you can touch it, you can measure it, you can go into it and be sheltered by it, and taste some of its material sweets!

Its spiritual fruits? Eternity alone will disclose how much Aberdeenshire owes, under God, to Reginald Radcliffe and James Turner.

Editor's Note

God is ready to work among us again. Are we ready to earnestly seek Him? Are we ready to put aside our church and denominational divisions and meet together in simple Christian unity and humility, confessing our sins, seeking God's forgiveness for our individual and national sins, and desiring God to send His Holy Spirit among us once again and change individuals, families, communities, and nations?

Do we really want to look to Him once again and live in holiness? Do we really want to see conversions and God glorified? As in past revivals, are we ready to see taverns closed for lack of business, crime and sin lessened, attendance in sports and theaters decline because of lack of interest, and hearts and conversations routinely engaged upon the things of God? Do you want to hate sin as God hates sin, and love others as Jesus did and does, giving His life for them, willing to be ridiculed and hated for living and proclaiming the truth and love of God in holiness?

Let us sincerely seek God once again, wholeheartedly desiring Him more than anything. Meet with your friends and pray for revival. Meet with your neighbors and pray for revival. Ask God to take away the sin and worldliness in your own heart. Ask Him to change and revive you so that you will serve Him single-mindedly and fully and so He will be glorified in and through you.

– Paul Miller

- *Wilt thou not revive us again: that thy people may rejoice in thee?* (Psalm 85:6)

- *Turn us again, O LORD God of hosts, cause thy face to shine; and we shall be saved.* (Psalm 80:19)

- *Draw nigh to God, and he will draw nigh to you. Cleanse your hands, ye sinners; and purify your hearts, ye double minded.* (James 4:8)

- *Elijah came unto all the people, and said, How long halt ye between two opinions? if the Lord be God, follow him: but if Baal, then follow him.* (1 Kings 18:21)

About the Author

John Shearer, M.A., was a Scottish author and minister most known for his contributions to Christian literature in the early 20th century. He is best recognized for his work *Old Time Revivals*, first published in 1927 by the World Wide Revival Prayer Movement of Atlantic City, New Jersey. This book offers a comprehensive account of various revivals throughout history, making it an indispensable overview of the greatest revivals of recent history.

Other Similar Titles

Words of Counsel
by Charles H. Spurgeon

Is there any occupation as profitable or rewarding as that of winning souls for Christ? It is a desirable employment, and the threshold for entry into this profession is set at a level any Christian may achieve – you must only love the Lord God with all your heart, soul, and mind; and your fellow man as yourself. This work is for all genuine Christians, of all walks of life. This is for you, fellow Christian.

Be prepared to be inspired, challenged, and convicted. Be prepared to weep, for the Holy Spirit may touch you deeply as you consider your coworkers, your neighbors, the children you know, and how much the Lord cares for these individuals. But you will also be equipped. Charles Spurgeon knew something about winning souls, and he holds nothing back as he shares biblical wisdom and practical application regarding the incredible work the Lord wants to do through His people to reach the lost.

Available where books are sold.

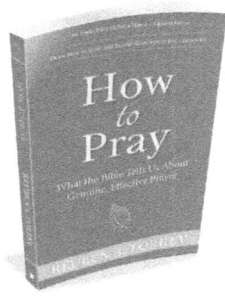

How to Pray
by Reuben A. Torrey

It is not necessary that the whole church prays to begin with. Great revivals always begin first in the hearts of a few men and women whom God arouses by His Spirit to believe in Him as a living God, as a God who answers prayer, and upon whose heart He lays a burden from which no rest can be found except in persistent crying unto God.

May God use this book to inspire many who are currently prayerless, or nearly so, to pray earnestly. May God stir up your own heart to be one of those burdened to pray, and to pray until God answers.

Available where books are sold.